For Jess Hernandez,
with deep gratitude.

Alithia Ramirez

Was an Artist

Alithia Ramirez Was an Artist

Michael Sampson Books
Dallas / New York
www.MichaelSampsonBooks.com
(972) 381-0009

A New Era in Publishing®

Publisher's Cataloging-In-Publication Data

Names: Lemay, Violet, author, illustrator. | Ramirez, Alithia, artist.
Title: Alithia Ramirez was an artist / written and illustrated by Violet Lemay ; including art by Alithia Ramirez
Description: Dallas ; New York : Michael Sampson Books, [2023] | Interest age level: 005-010. |
Summary: Alithia Ramirez dreamed of studying art in Paris. She drew the world as it should be--full of color and joy, creativity and fun. From her teachers to her family and friends, Alitha shared her gifts with an open heart. Being an artist is never easy, but she drew every day to practice her skills and help everyone feel the love that art can bring. Written to honor Alithia and all the lives affected by the Uvalde school tragedy, Alithia Ramirez Was an Artist will help preserve the memory of this talented young girl through her story and her artwork.--Publisher.
Identifiers: ISBN: 978-1-61254-649-0 (hardcover)
Subjects: LCSH: Ramirez, Alithia--Juvenile literature. | Child artists--Texas--Uvalde--Biography-- Juvenile literature. | Victims of crimes--Texas--Uvalde--Biography--Juvenile literature. | Art--Juvenile literature. | Art appreciation--Juvenile literature. | Sharing--Juvenile literature. | Goal (Psychology)--Juvenile literature. | CYAC: Ramirez, Alithia. | Artists--Texas--Uvalde-- Biography. | Victims of crimes--Texas--Uvalde--Biography. | Art. | Art appreciation. | Sharing. | Goal. | LCGFT: Biographies. | BISAC: JUVENILE NONFICTION / Art / General. | JUVENILE NONFICTION / Biography & Autobiography / Art.
Classification: LCC: N6537.R2376 L46 2023 | DDC: 709.2--dc23

This book has been officially leveled by using the F&P Text Level GradientTM Leveling System.

ISBN 978-1-61254-649-0
LCCN 2023933234

Printed in China
10 9 8 7 6 5 4 3 2 1

For more information or to contact the author, please go to
www.AlithiasArtAngels.com.

Alithia Ramirez

Was an Artist

Written and
Illustrated by
Violet Lemay

Including Art by
Alithia Ramirez

Michael Sampson
books

Alithia Ramirez was an artist.

Even when she was a baby,
her art could not
be contained.

As a toddler, Alithia's art was **bold.**

Expressive.

All over the place.

As she grew up, Alithia was always surrounded by crayons, markers, colored pencils, and paints (especially acrylics).

Also adoring fans.

Her art supplies were popular, so Alithia kept them safe. But even the most devoted artist forgets to clean up sometimes.

Still, sharing her skills came naturally.

Being an artist wasn't always easy though. Sometimes, making art was frustrating.

Alithia saw this:

But she drew this:

Her hands couldn't always keep up with her eyes, but Alithia never stayed frustrated or discouraged. She just took a break and then kept drawing.

After all, Alithia wasn't a **camera**.

Alithia Ramirez was an artist.

Alithia drew her teachers.

She drew her classmates.

She drew her family.

And of course,
like all great artists,
Alithia Ramirez
drew herself.

She drew when she was happy···

and when she was sad.

Alithia had big art plans and big art dreams.
She drew toward those plans and dreams . . .
always creating, always hoping,
always dreaming.

She drew the world as it should be:

full of *jOY* and COLOR,
full of **LOVE** and **peace**.

Alithia Ramirez was an artist.
Her voice was in her heart and in her hands.
Her voice came out on paper.

It went like this:

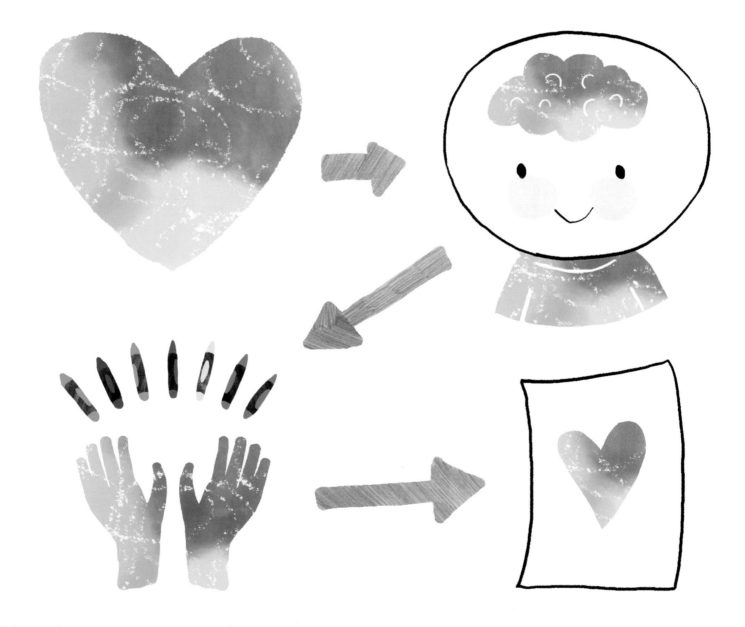

The Artist's Voice in Action
(a scientific rendering*)

*Some studies include the eyes!

Heart ⟶ Head ⟶ Hands ⟶ Paper

Alithia's art voice was beautiful. Powerful. That's not surprising, because . . .

Alithia's art voice was **LOVE.**

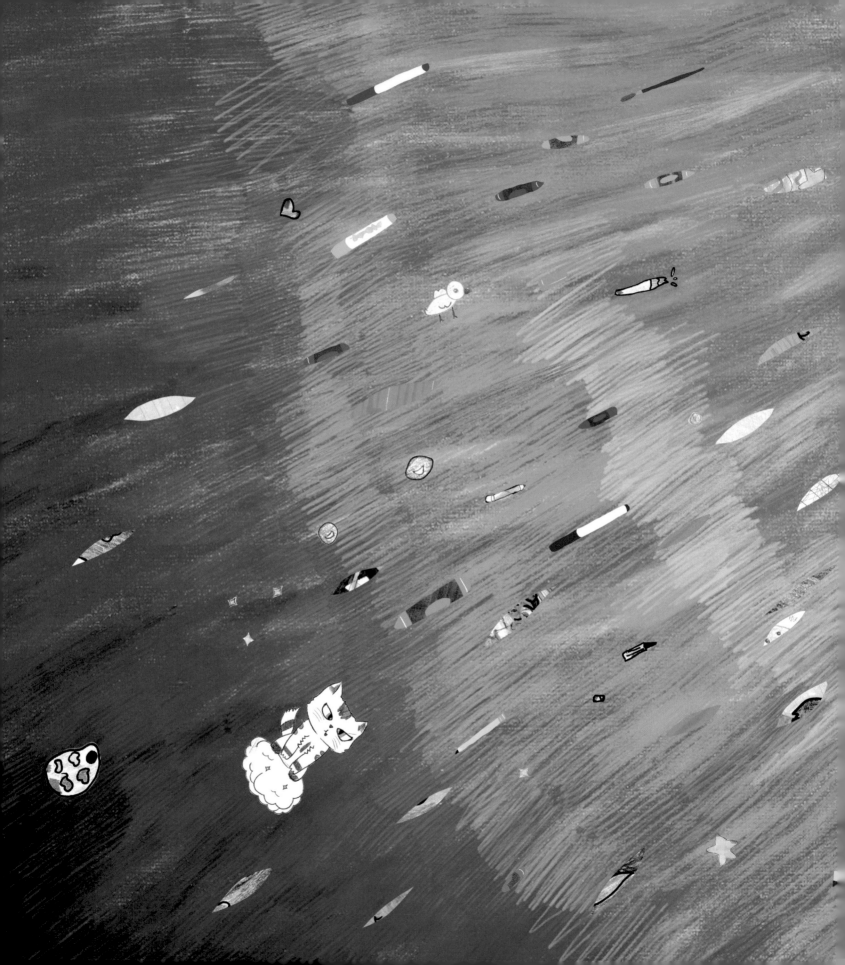

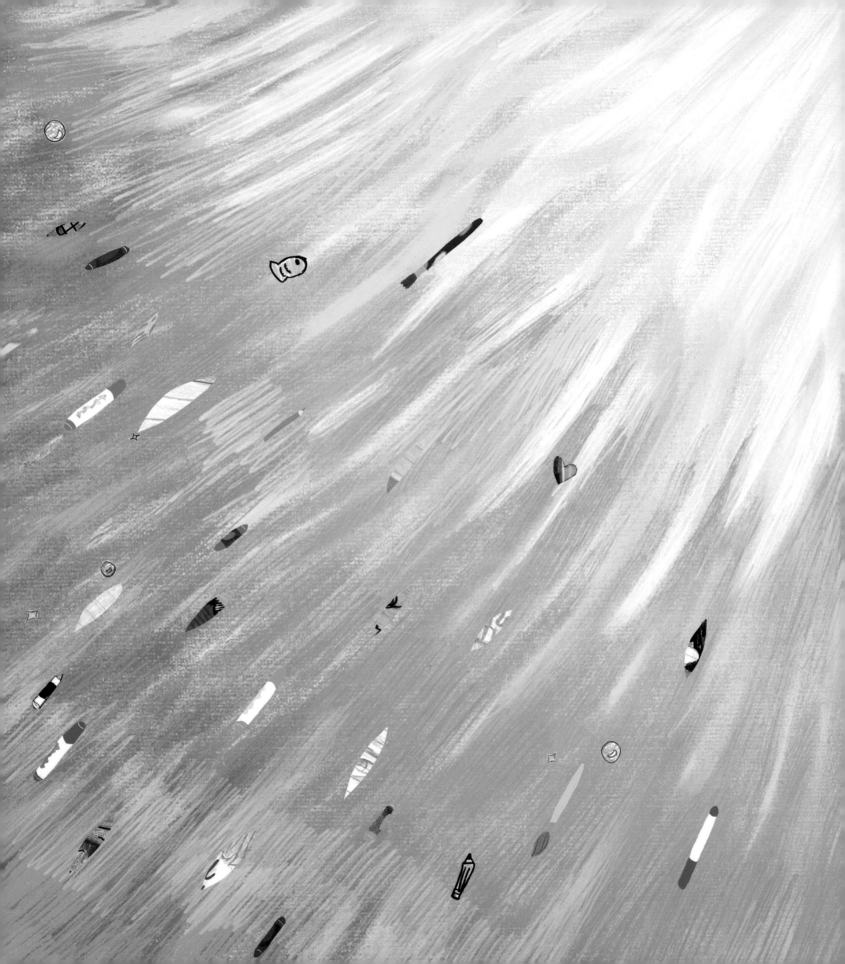

When an artist dies, her art lives on.
Alithia's art lives in all of us . . .
and Alithia lives in our hearts.

Author's Note

I never knew Alithia Ramirez, but based on what everyone says about her, she and I have a lot in common. We are both artists.

This book was written with the support of Alithia Ramirez's parents, Jess Hernandez and Ryan Ramirez, in response to the school tragedy in Uvalde, Texas, on May 24, 2022. I hope it can bring small comfort to Alithia's family and friends, and to anyone whose life has been affected by gun violence. Proceeds from sales of *Alithia Ramirez Was an Artist* will go to the Alithia Haven Ramirez Memorial Summer Seminar Scholarship fund.

Artists use art to celebrate, to love, to unite humanity, and to change the world. The world needs your art voice! **Share your creations at AlithiasArtAngels.com.**

Art Citations

Violet Lemay, who illustrated this book, took great care to recreate Alithia's self-portrait, family portrait, and her horse and chicken drawings. All of the other works of art shown on this page were created by Alithia Ramirez and are reproduced in this book with permission from her parents. Violet used Photoshop to incorporate scans of Alithia's original drawings into her illustrations.

Alithia Ramirez

Let's Talk

When she was very young, Alithia wanted to be a nurse; but by the time she was four years old, she had changed her mind. From then on, she wanted to be an artist. What do you want to be when you grow up?

According to her dad, Alithia's favorite art supply was "whatever lasted the longest." What are your favorite art supplies? What new ones would you like to try?

When Alithia was discouraged with her art, her mom told her to never give up. So Alithia would take a break and then keep drawing. Are you ever frustrated when you draw? What's a good way to handle frustration?

Alithia's self-portrait looks different than photos of her. Does that matter? How is a drawing or a painting different from the art of photography?

Alithia drew this work of art when she was very sad, as a gift. She gave it away to make someone feel better. How can making art help you when you feel sad? How can you use art to cheer up someone who is sad or simply to show your love?

Alithia's dream was to study art in Paris. What are your hopes and dreams?